TWILIGHT ON THE NARROW GAUGE

RIO GRANDE SCENES OF THE FIFTIES

BY FREDERICK A. KRAMER

Photography by John Krause

Other Quadrant Press Review Titles:

No. 1 STREAMLINED STEAM (out of print)
By Eric Archer ________________________ $2.95

No. 2 THE MILWAUKEE ROAD UNDER WIRE (out of print)
By Karl Zimmermann ________________________ $2.95

No. 3 ERIE-LACKAWANNA EAST
By Karl Zimmermann ________________________ $3.95

No. 4 ACROSS NEW YORK BY TROLLEY
By Frederick A. Kramer ________________________ $3.95

No. 6 THE REMARKABLE GG1
By Karl Zimmermann ________________________ $4.75

No. 7 MOTIVE POWER OF THE JERSEY CENTRAL
By Michael Eagleson ________________________ $4.75

QUADRANT PRESS, INC.
19 West 44th Street
New York, N. Y. 10036
Phone (212) 490-1622

ISBN-0-915276-14-3

©1976
By Frederick A. Kramer

Cover photograph by Victor Hand

INTRODUCTION

COLORADO'S mountains — capped by snow and cloud and sunlight — once held their wealth of precious metals and mineral treasures in high seclusion. Hazard and hardship accompanied all who passed upon the mountain barrier, for these were the Rocky Mountains, the challenge of Colorado.

The front ranges addressed the westward migrants with unbroken majesty. Among the high passes, useful crossing points were few. The only complete penetration of the front ranges was the Arkansas River canyon through the Royal Gorge.

Behind these ranges lay broad highland meadows called parks, and beyond the parks loomed still more mountains. It was there in central Colorado that the backbone of the Rockies was found. Down the Mosquito Range wound the Continental Divide, crossing in back of the Collegiate peaks, conceding Monarch and Marshall Passes, until finally it veered southwest in search of the rugged San Juans.

In a span of four generations, man brought greater change to those mountains than had all the ages since the outbursts of nature which formed them. Transportation was an essential element in that change, and rail transportation was the most significant part of the picture.

Engineering triumphs were many in building narrow gauge rail lines into scenic, lonely, and sometimes frightening country. And then it was asking a lot to operate pony-sized machinery on steep grades and in places where a few miles or a few minutes could bring an overwhelming change in the weather, a chance of being stranded. But the name of the game was silver.

The free coinage of silver had brought unprecedented prosperity to the mining enterprises. Rugged individualists wrenched ore from the lodes as fast as the mines could be driven. No man asked "What was your name in the States?" for this was runaway-begin-again, start-your-fortune frontier. Where the mines were, the rails went. Windy Point, Jack's Cabin, Dallas Divide, and St. Elmo were waypoints on the route to riches.

The bonanza vanished abruptly in 1893 when free coinage was repealed. Despite the "cross of gold" speeches by William Jennings Bryan, national policy did not again provide the incentive to thrust still more railroads through wild grandeur in search of silver. The secular decline soon began and continued until both mining works and narrow gauge operations were decimated.

The automobile, the Depression, and advancing years also thrust themselves upon the marginal railroad economy. What little was left depended for its existence on mountain isolation. Little more than an exuberant post-war decade's highway construction was needed to deal with that.

Into this last phase of the genuine nineteenth century article moved John Krause, his Speed Graphic in hand. He hiked, he climbed, he waded, and did whatever else was necessary to find the better camera angle. And then he waited for the proper moment. This pictorial review captures some of those moments. The end of the glory days was at hand, and they cast their *Twilight on the Narrow Gauge.*

CONTENTS

FRONT COVER:
Pressing westward out of Chama, 483 tosses a smoky turbulence into the San Juan wilderness.

INSIDE FRONT COVER:
October fifth, 1954 — the last time a Rio Grande crew ran a train through the mesa country at Elk Creek.

THIS PAGE:
Dawn at Gunnison. Two 480 series locomotives make ready for one of railroading's most fabled runs, a stock train over Marshall Pass.

INSIDE BACK COVER:
From the crags of Windy Point where only eagles dare to perch, Wolf Creek valley's mountain pasture stretches down toward Chama.

A lonely vastness spreads across the 10,000 foot elevations that crest the San Juans' eastern slope. This panorama looks east near Cumbres Pass. One of Colorado's last frontiers, it is a land of evergreen and aspen accustomed to the snow that has persisted into April of 1954. Helper engine 493 with a refrigerator car and a box car holds the main. The box car serves as a vantage point for the brakeman on the roof as he observes the movement of a cut of cars on Los Pinos siding.

INITIAL development of the mountain region could not be supported by the existing Indian trails. Those primitive trails were helpful, however, in exploring and in suggesting where practical routes could be developed. In exploration and development, no man contributed more to southwestern Colorado than an orphaned Russian immigrant, Otto Mears. He was a trusted friend of the Indians and a vigorous entrepreneur.

Mears started early in the wagon freighting business using available trails. Great difficulties were involved and as a result, Mears expanded into the road building business. Over the years, he built a series of toll roads, some of which significantly affected railroad affairs which followed. Mears truly earned his sobriquet: he was the Pathfinder of the San Juans.

Wagon roads, however, could not support a fully productive economy. Railroads were needed, as was well recognized, for they had reached the eastern edge of the Rockies in easy, competitive venture. The dilemma was how to penetrate narrow canyons, run tight circles among the mountains, and cling high upon the brows and slopes. The assault of steel rails upon the mountain citadel was limited by the technology of the day and the tremendous costs involved.

Into this situation came General William Jackson Palmer — ex-cavalryman, railroad builder, and a man completely capable of dealing in terms of empire. He planned initially to build south to Santa Fe and perhaps into Mexico using narrow gauge. His railroad was to be the first important common carrier to adopt a three-foot spacing between the rails, just as the rest of the nation had squarely settled on a standard of 4-feet, 8½ inches. Others watched while Palmer proceeded.

General Palmer's railroad was the Denver & Rio Grande. It headed south from Denver toward the Rio Grande country of its name in 1871. By 1872, the rails reached Pueblo where Palmer organized the Central Colorado Improvement Company.

The Improvement Company was intended to create an industrial city south of town. In a decade it would be reorganized as the Colorado Coal & Iron Company, an industrial giant that would be the Rio Grande's principal traffic producer for the next seventy-five years.

Grand as they were, Palmer's plans came to a halt with the Panic of '73. Construction funds could not be raised then or for the next few years. But when conditions eased and Palmer was ready to start south again, he found that the local citizens had helped the Atchison, Topeka & Santa Fe to occupy Raton Pass, the only practical route in the area. He had lost by a hair's breadth.

West was the way to turn. Palmer saw silver booms in full swing at both Silverton and Leadville. So it was up the Sangre de Cristo Range and over Veta Pass with the three foot rails, reaching Alamosa in 1878. Ahead lay the San Juans with Silverton snuggled in one of the innermost crypts. An alternate route to Santa Fe might yet be found from Alamosa should Mexico again become an attractive goal. But other matters had meanwhile brought the Rio Grande to the crisis stage.

Palmer's route to Leadville was up the Arkansas River canyon. That route through the Royal Gorge was so narrow that only one railroad could be built at certain points. Once again with the help of local citizens, the Atchison, Topeka & Santa Fe construction crews already occupied the sites. This time, however, the locations had been previously surveyed and claimed by the Rio Grande.

After considerable mayhem, the matter went to court. A lower court decision favored the Santa Fe and that ended Palmer's borrowing ability for the time being. It also jeopardized the holdings of Rio Grande investors who consequently pressed Palmer to protect their investments. Hemmed in, Palmer leased the Rio Grande to the Santa Fe on December 13, 1878 and awaited further developments.

He had not long to wait. The U. S. Supreme Court decided in Palmer's favor on April 21, 1879 and Colorado courts ordered the lease with the Santa Fe terminated shortly thereafter. Palmer was back in charge of the Rio Grande, but it had become a finacial mess that went into the hands of a Receiver that July. Not the least of the problems was the division of Rio Grande traffic between the Santa Fe and the Union Pacific. A subtler contest would now begin: enter Jay Gould.

Gould was a financier who controlled the Union Pacific. He was close to gaining control of the Denver, South Park & Pacific, a narrow gauge line that ex-Governor John Evans had formed in 1873. That profitable line headed southwest from Denver more or less directly toward Leadville where it would soon be challenging the Rio Grande for traffic. Moreover, the Pacific part of the South Park's corporate title indicated their intention to continue southwest into and beyond the San Juans. Further conflict with the Rio Grande seemed likely.

Gould took the opportunity to buy Rio Grande securities at depressed prices and by agreement with Palmer, sat on the Rio Grande board of directors. Gould thus projected himself into a position of being able to directly resolve the potentially destructive conflicts between the Rio Grande and the South Park.

Gould's position also gave him the power to resolve the remaining quarrels between the Rio Grande and the Santa Fe. He did that by the indirect means of threatening economic reprisals against the Santa Fe. Under that pressure, the Santa Fe agreed to stay out of Denver and Leadville in return for the Rio Grande keeping out of New Mexico. The Rio Grande agreed to pay for the road work that

Down Durango way, 488 adds the aroma of coal smoke to the fragrance of mesquite. The La Plata Range, dominant in the background, will be left behind as the train steps south to Farmington from this point near Carbon Junction.

the Santa Fe had done in the direction of Leadville and both roads consented to drop all remaining court suits.

As between the Rio Grande and the South Park, Gould set roles and objectives for each. The Rio Grande was to extend their lines into the silver, coal, iron, and timber areas so as to develop the region. This was just what Palmer had wanted for his Pueblo operations. With peace and Jay Gould at hand, Palmer could again raise new capital in the money markets.

The objective for the South Park was to cross the Continental Divide into the promising Gunnison country and thence build westward. This was the transcontinental flavor that was to Jay Gould's liking, in contrast to the local role he had handed Palmer. The matter of selecting a route over the Divide was critical and it was on this point that the fatal error occurred. The South Park's engineers deemed Marshall Pass unsuitable. It was that judgment that would ultimately cost Gould the Colorado empire he had wrought.

After some deliberation, the South Park decided to cross the Divide by means of a tunnel under Altman Pass. This was to be the heroic, colorful Alpine Tunnel that deserved its superlatives but took too much time to build. During its construction, Palmer built well over 800 miles of narrow gauge, a program that used a great deal of outside financing. Gould put his money into the South Park and in so doing, did not participate in the increased financial base of the Rio Grande. His holdings lost their leverage and he could no longer control Palmer.

Gratitude did not overwhelm General Palmer. Seeing another chance to control his destiny, he persuaded Otto Mears to sell his toll road over Marshall Pass. The Rio Grande used the nearly-new alignment that Mears had built to good advantage.

The Rio Grande reached Gunnison in 1881, a year ahead of the South Park, and pushed right on into the Black Canyon en route to the Great Salt Lake. Although the South Park eventually finished and operated Alpine Tunnel, it was essentially worthless. Gould had suffered a major loss.

1881 was also the year in which Palmer decided to standard gauge the principal Rio Grande routes as a means of remaining competitive. There was, of course, the converse of that decision. What was to remain narrow gauge would become increasingly more isolated: geographically, technologically, commercially. It would take many years, but the die had been cast. Thus southwestern Colorado became the focal point of what narrow gauge survived longest, and thereby the attention of this book.

In 1925, the Rio Grande placed an order with Baldwin Locomotive Works, their first order with that builder in a dozen years. The result was the 480 series, class K36, a small standard gauge design fitted onto narrow gauge wheel sets. The ten 2-8-2 Mikados were highly successful workhorses. None of this series was scrapped until 1955, and even then it was only because the 485 had been run into the turntable pit at Salida. Wishing to repeat the success of the 480s, the Rio Grande converted six light engines they had on hand in 1928 from standard gauge to narrow gauge. This produced class K37, Mikados numbered in the 490 series. The conversion was also successful and four more engines were converted in 1930. The 496 was equipped so that it could also couple directly to standard gauge cars, the only instance of this capability on the narrow gauge.

487 and 494 fill Monero canyon with thunder in May, 1953.

494
Rio Grande

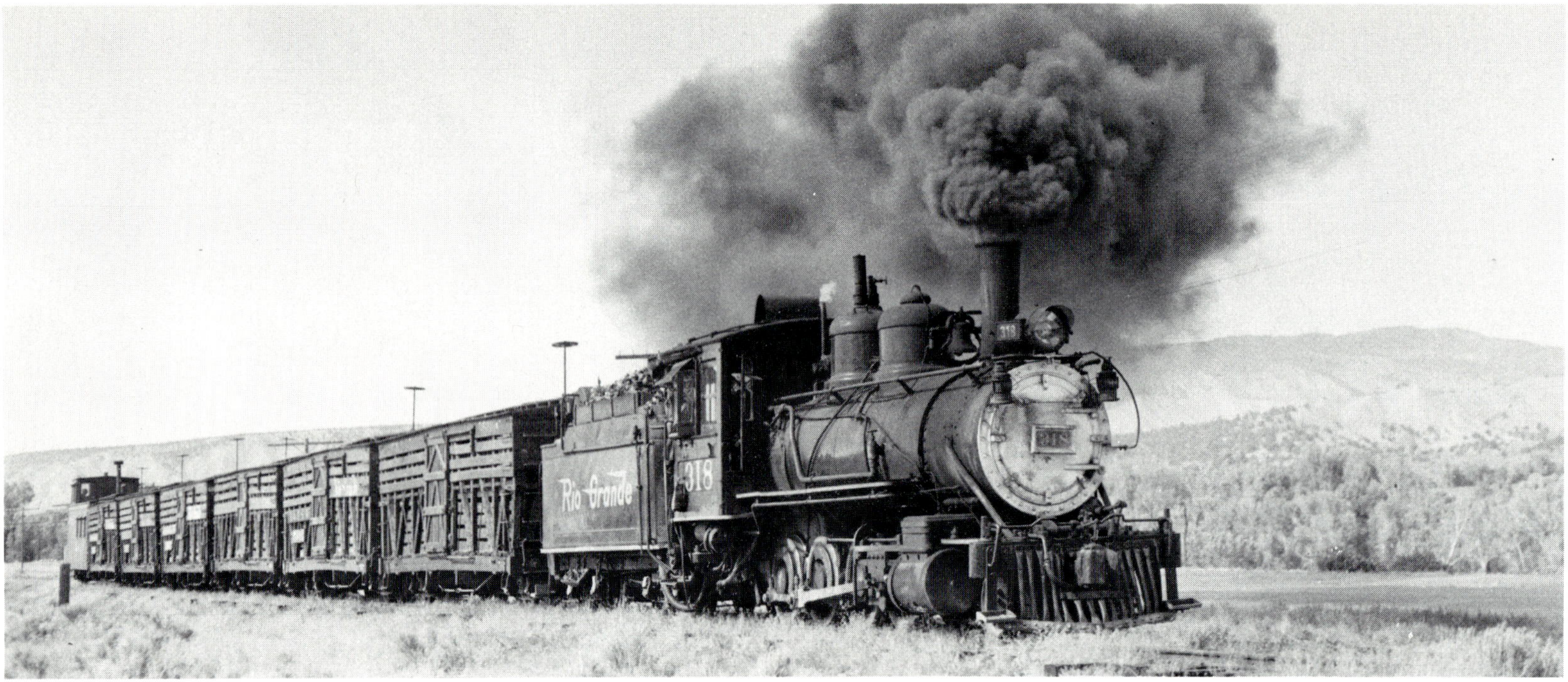
Rio Grande
318

454
454
Rio Grande

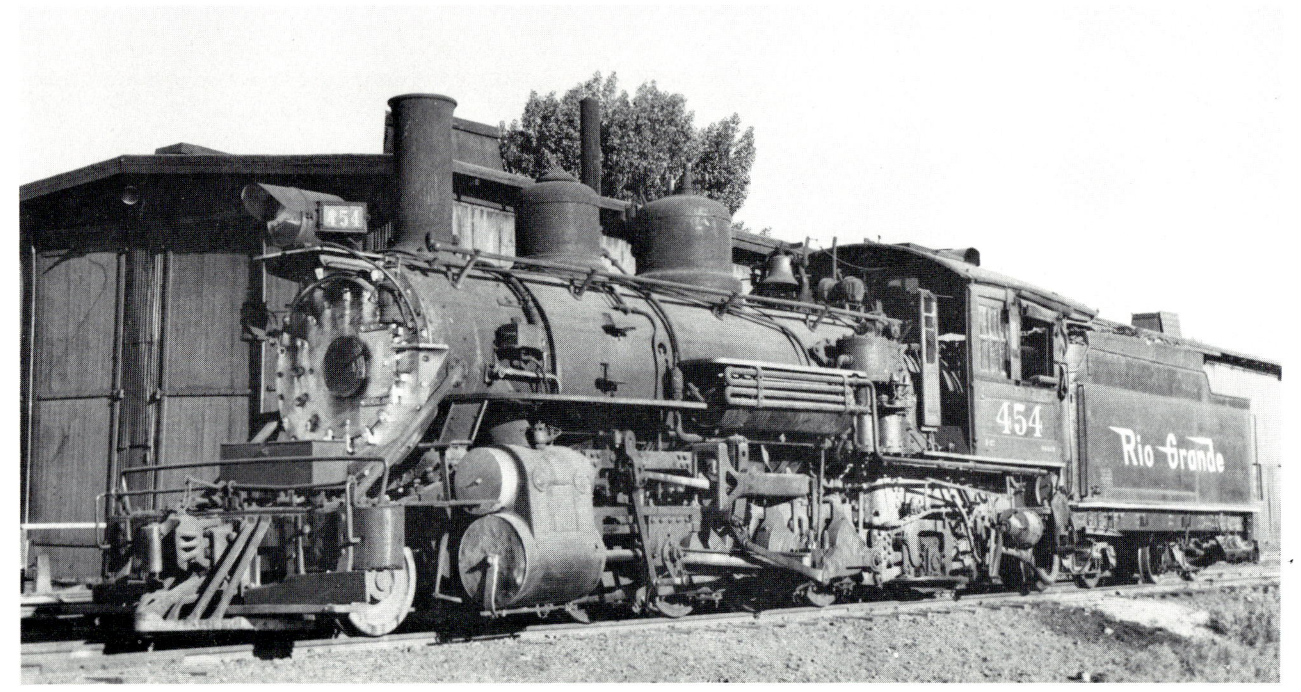

Class C18 was a group of 2-8-0 Consolidations for use on lightly built branch lines. Five of the class came from the defunct Florence & Cripple Creek in 1917. After another three decades of service, 317 and 318 were combined into one good engine and road number 318 was continued. The 450–464 series was built by Baldwin in 1903. These were the first Mikados and they became class K27. Their outside frame design gave them a better stability than the inside-frame Consolidations in the event of a derailment. This stability, with a tendency to scoot along the ties when off the track, earned them the nickname "mudhens." Class K28 was a group of ten Mikados built by American Locomotive Company in 1923 and numbered in the 470 series. Intended as passenger power over the passes, they were dubbed "sport models." Most of the class was conscripted by Uncle Sam in 1943 for duty on the White Pass & Yukon in Alaska. Only 473, 476, and 478 got deferments.

South of Montrose, 318 hurries for an appointment with some sheep at Ridgway. Mudhen 454 stays at Montrose, basking beside the two-stall enginehouse.

Mixed train in tow, 476 follows the cliffs at Rockwood on the Silverton line. The narrow gauge could curve on the brim of a sombrero.

SWITCHBACK AT MONARCH

Facing away from Monarch Pass, this general view looks east across the quarry operation. The tracks in the foreground are level, but the approach from the left is still quite steep. Helper engine 480 and the caboose wait there during loading, a process already completed for the half of the train set out on the siding. No. 481 patiently spots each empty gondola under the loading chute. The cuts of cars will then be joined and pulled forward where the train will turn on a wye so that the locomotives face downgrade. Railroading was suspended each winter, generally starting in January for about three months. During this period, enough limestone was blasted from the slopes to last until the following winter. The snow lingers but the snowplow attachments have been removed in this May, 1953 view. And oh, how that wind does blow.

MONARCH PASS lies on a direct line between Royal Gorge on the east and the Black Canyon on the west. An ideal location, yet Otto Mears, the South Park engineers, and General Palmer all avoided it.

The difficulty with Monarch Pass was not its height, since its 11,312 foot elevation was typical of the continuous mountain barrier in the area. Indeed, Alpine Tunnel was built 200 feet higher.

It was the necessity of finding a way to gain altitude slowly that determined if a pass would be suitable for a railroad. Only the Union Pacific found the ultimate: a moderate, direct grade at Sherman Hill. That route, 200 miles to the north, was as favorable as any railroad would find over the Rockies.

Typically, however, it was necessary to locate a line so that it would loop among a series of rising crests, each loop gaining altitude toward the pass. Marshall Pass is an excellent example of crossing by this method.

Unfortunately, Monarch was at the head of a narrow, steep canyon. The last place to loop was above Maysville where a great double hairpin was needed. Then, in the steepness of the canyon at Garfield, it became necessary to switchback.

A switchback is the last resort for operating with adhesion type locomotives. The process is to proceed past a trailing switch and then continue the journey by backing up, as if onto a siding. Actually, the siding is a continuation of the line itself as it climbs along the same side of the canyon. The reverse movements involved were time-consuming and only one train of limited length could operate at a time.

The Monarch branch had a double switchback. It was built in 1883 to reach gold and silver mines near the pass. No transcontinental intentions were involved, for Marshall Pass was already in successful service. Railroading outlasted those mining ventures that had justified such extreme construction by virtue of the high quality limestone found high up in the canyon. The quarried stone was brought down the mountain in narrow gauge cars for transfer to standard gauge cars at Salida. From there, the stone moved to the Colorado Fuel & Iron Company's steel mills at Minnequa, just south of Pueblo.

The continuing importance of the limestone resource warranted converting the branch to standard gauge in the summer of 1956. To do so cost $431,000, but the economies of diesel standardization and direct shipments had spoken.

A maintenance-of-way crew unloads cinders on the first hairpin curve of the Maysville loop. The watercourse beneath 483 is the South Arkansas River, flowing downward right-to-left. In the foreground, US 50 climbs in the opposite direction.

The climb toward the second hairpin is steep. Although the train is far above the highway, motorists are so close to the grade crossing that the warning painted on the highway is in the picture. The fill leading to the grade crossing can be seen left of the top edge of the plow. Plows were attached in the late Fall and generally removed during April. By then they had served their dual function of snow removal and shunting aside rocks that snow plus freeze-and-thaw had sent down on the tracks.

By 1950, the heaviest motive power assignments were needed on the Alamosa-Durango line, not the old mainline out of Salida. Since the 480 series were adequate for Monarch branch service, they were brought to Salida except for 484 and 488. Two engines would work a train of 52 empties to Maysville. The train was then cut in half and brought to the switchback where each engine would separately handle a half of the remaining cars. 481 and 485, above and below Garfield respectively, lead their 26-car cuts and their helpers toward the switchback.

Action is nearly complete at the lower switchback. The train has been cut in half again, the lead engine has backed its thirteen cars up this grade to the right, the 480 has pushed the remaining thirteen cars around the curve seen in the foreground and onto the stub track out of the picture to the left. Now, caboose-first and throttle valve wide open, the backward blast up the 4½ percent grade commences.

Three views at the upper switchback. Top right, **481** completes the last step of the ascent as it shoves the empties up to the left. At left, **480** holds at the clearance point sign for a switch alignment on a down trip. The helper has gone down light. Above, **481** returns for the second half of a loaded train, the first half having been left on the stub of the lower switchback.

SEPTEMBER'S mellow days opened the livestock shipping season. Fatted from a summer's grazing, the herds of cattle and flocks of sheep were gathered from the high places. Some were chosen for market, others for movement to winter pasture.

The narrow gauge was well equipped to handle this seasonal traffic. Stock pens were located throughout the territory, frequently at sidings in isolated country. From these points the stockyard journey or the winter sojourn would begin and, for those that pastured over, these would be the return points when late Spring arrived.

Hundreds of narrow gauge stock cars were built to handle the livestock rush. Most of the fleet was a part of the 1903–1904 equipment expansion, the rest came during a mid-1920s improvement program. Even after major abandonments in 1954, an amazing total of 353 stock cars still survived. Many of these were cut down for service in the then profitable pipe trains.

Other freight was not moved in stock trains because it was important to complete the trips quickly. The Rio Grande assigned as many as four locomotives to a train, the only regular service in which that was done. Delays, if encountered, would require a stop to give the animals proper care. The drovers and stockmen who would be needed for watering and handling rode along in the caboose.

By the 1950s, stock shipments had little impact on operating revenues. What little traffic the shippers cared to offer was not particularly desired under the circumstances at hand. Shipments became increasingly sporadic and meagre until, finally, abandonment took place.

It's Friday, September 11, 1953. A cattle shipment will be made this day from the pens at Parlin. The stock arrives in the custody of the riders and crosses the tracks oblivious of the helper engine waiting west of the tank. Opposite: the fellows with the Stetsons have the holding pens full and the brakemen are ready for their chores to get the cars spotted for loading two-at-a-time.

By mid-afternoon, the loading was nearly done. The only cattle remaining to be loaded are in the lower right corner in front of the cowboy who is wheeling his horse. The cut of empty cars blocks the main and follows the curve of the siding toward the chutes. Things are working out just fine: there'll be a few extra cars, but not too many to leave on the siding. The helper is up front now, ready for double heading duty. Opposite: a brakeman's-eye view of the chute shows the natural balkiness of the animals. The beevo in front casts a baleful eye, apparently not wishing to visit the government inspector down Denver way.

The double header completes the twelve miles to Sargent. Two other engines of the 480 series have been sent over from Salida, turned on the wye, and wait to be cut into the middle of the train. Then double-headed and double-helpered, the stock train trots out of Sargent on the long climb to Marshall Pass. Smoke from a four-engine train fills this valley, an event that was destined to occur only once more — ever.

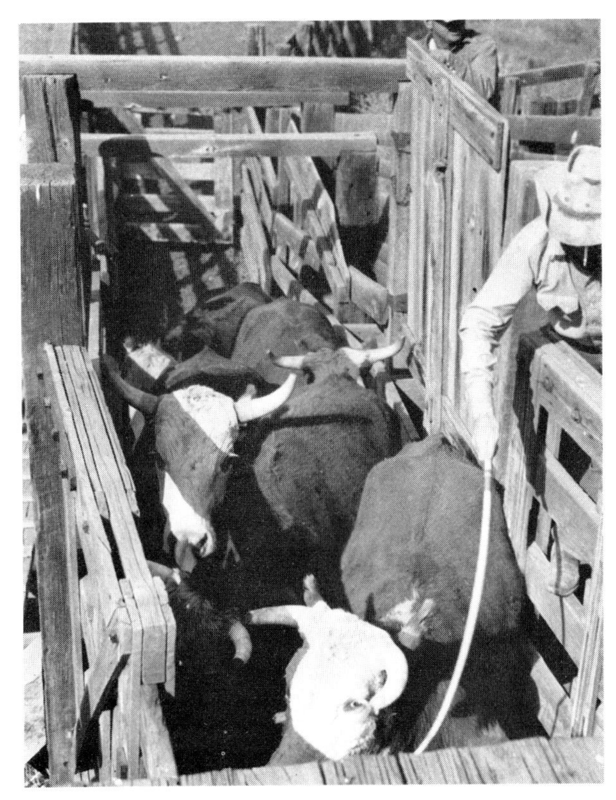

A stock car movement pauses at Jack's Cabin for water. The double deck arrangement inside the car accommodates the shipment of sheep.

318 handles a sheep train being loaded from the Denver & Rio Grande pens at Ridgway. The view looks toward Ouray in August of 1952.

The last chance to witness long strings of stock cars rocking
along the old mainline west of Gunnison came in 1954.
Reminiscent of the glory days of stock handling, these were
clean-up trains bringing in the idle cars. Headed by 268, a
string of slat-sided refugees jangles east in mesa country.
There'll be no cattle to load from the chute at Iola, but a
young lad has crossed over from the Big Little Store to climb
up and watch the train pass. He made a memory for himself.

WATER & COAL STOPS

STEAM locomotives operated on a non-condensing thermodynamic cycle. On the Rio Grande narrow gauge, two factors worked in the direction of requiring frequent stops to replenish the supply of water for the boiler. One was the relatively small cubic capacity of the tenders and the other was the continuous steaming demands at full power on the lengthy grades.

The water tanks themselves stood like silent sentinels in the wilderness. Exact locations were fixed by the need for a consistent water supply and a relatively level approach on which to stop and re-start the trains. Locations able to take advantage of a gravity feed for the tank offered an important added benefit.

Coaling facilities frequently took the form of trestles upon which gondola loads of coal could be pushed, then emptied into pockets that held the coal until it was released into the tenders by gravity. An alternative means of elevating the coal into the storage pockets was by the use of hoisting mechanisms, a method usually restricted the busiest of places, such as those where there was an enginehouse. The last resort was available in emergencies at any waypoint: having the crew shovel the coal into the tender from a gondola stationed on an adjacent track.

A water stop at Mears Junction in May, 1955. No. 489 heads a load of scrap rail cars toward the Baldwin branch.

487 pulls into the servicing area at Antonito. This **1955** scene shows the trestle-type coaling facility which was replaced the following year by a moveable conveyor-type coal loader. The water tank at trainside was badly damaged by freezing in the winter of **1966**.

A freight from Alamosa drifts past the double-spouted tank and on into Chama yard. At the left of the picture, four tank cars have been spotted at the oil loading racks.

The Parlin tank sat next to the creek, west of the sidings and maintenance structures. For nearly thirty years, the old South Park line ran parallel to the Rio Grande between Gunnison and Parlin, then headed northeast to cross the Divide at Alpine Tunnel. By 1910 when Alpine was abandoned, the Colorado & Southern was successor to the old South Park. Their trackage west of the tunnel became isolated. By an exchange of leases, the Rio Grande operated the Parlin-Quartz section of the Alpine approach as well as the C&S Baldwin branch. In return, Colorado & Southern operated the Rio Grande's Blue River branch. In 1911, the Rio Grande built a half a mile of connecting track at Parlin, but Colorado & Southern delayed dismantling the unused parallel rails until 1923.

Below, its the helper's turn for water at Gato, forty-six miles west of Chama. May, 1953.

On Saturday, May 21, 1955, No. 268 was sent from Gunnison to Marshall Pass on a rescue mission. The object was to bring in the **489** and a string of gondolas which had been delivered at Poncha Junction on the day before. The **489**'s journey up to the pass was delayed by snow and rocks on the track to the extent that very little water remained in the tender as they approached the tank east of Marshall Pass. Unfortunately, that tank was frozen and there wasn't enough left to reach the tank on the west side. So the fire was dumped and the engine crew walked down to Sargent — a 14 mile hike!

The fireman on 268 handles the spout control chain on the tank at Gunnison. View is from the coal tower.

The coal tower and steam heating plant stack dominate the lower end of Salida yard. No. **483** prepares for a Monarch branch assignment. Note the three-rail crossover at the right edge of the picture. Left: No. 1166, the standard gauge switcher at Salida, and **489** on the move adjacent to the standpipe supplied from the tank at right.

A gondola tops the coaling trestle at Sargent.

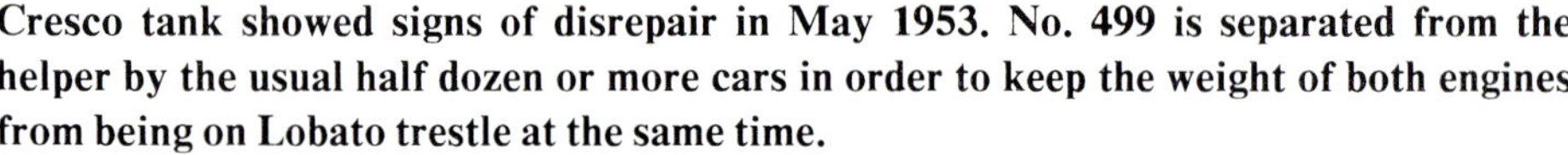

Cresco tank showed signs of disrepair in May 1953. No. 499 is separated from the helper by the usual half dozen or more cars in order to keep the weight of both engines from being on Lobato trestle at the same time.

Top right: the track folds around Los Pinos tank, makes a tight right turn and comes out where 493 is seen backing a caboose and two cars up from the siding. Right: the steel tank at La Jara was a replacement. Like the old wooden design, the access ladder had panels that swung over the lower steps and locked so as to discourage the adventurous.

The coal tower was a prominent skyline feature of the yards at Chama. Gondola cars are seen on the unloading ramp that served the coal hoist. From this position, sand could be unloaded into its supply pen. Ash pit and ash service functions took place on the other side.

A double header passes the coal tipple at Monero. Trucks unloaded at the top.

Eastbound from Cumbres, the tracks round the shoulder of land from which this picture was taken and enter a great loop built through the broad meadow. This is Tanglefoot Curve. One engine handles the train when descending, all helpers being sent back light. Train lengths ran as high as 70 cars on this segment and as high as 100 between Antonito and Alamosa. There are 67 freight cars this trip: 10 lumber, 36 box, 7 tank, 8 gondolas, 6 pipe cars, plus the caboose. Snow still lingers in this high country during May of 1953.

STATIONS & STRUCTURES

A classic beauty, this Victorian gem at Crested Butte. Although "the Butte" was known for lead, zinc, and deep snow, the mainstay of the economy was the coking coal that was mined for Colorado Fuel & Iron's mills at Minnequa. The coal traffic sustained not only the branch, but indeed the entire Marshall Pass operation in the final years.

IN THE COURSE of carving his Colorado empire, General Palmer brooked no nonsense from the town fathers of existing settlements when be built his lines into untapped territory. Whatever petty wrangles and minor concessions he may have saved himself, Palmer paid a high enough price in the early years of expansion.

It was the local offended citizenry of Trinidad who helped the Santa Fe secure Raton Pass because Palmer had terminated in a new town called El Moro, an inconvenient five miles north. Similarly, Palmer angered the locals in Canon City by stopping an inconvenient distance east of town. They acted against Palmer in his Royal Gorge battle.

Even though these actions contributed to his temporary loss of control of the Rio Grande, Palmer didn't mend his ways when he returned to build the Rio Grande westward. At Conejos, the tracks just seemed to miss town by a mile and a place named Antonito sprang into being. When the rails later crossed the wilderness to reach the Animas River, Palmer created a new place called Durango. This sorely upset the folks in adjacent Animas City, but they never had a revenge as handsome as the people of Trinidad or Canon City.

However, most place names were merely waypoints, tank towns, or sidings needed for the telegraphic dispatch of railroad operations. By and large, the station points were served by frame buildings, although some interesting exceptions existed. By 1955, what had not been abandoned earlier would be closed within the next few years.

Antonito in Studebaker days; Sapinero in its final years; and Poncha Junction when only Monarch trains ran by.

La Jara, meaning *rock rose* in Spanish, boasted a stucco finish above the ground level clapboard facing on both station and freighthouse. The Rio Grande emblem is attached between the second story window and the balcony.

ALLISON

DULCE
WESTERN UNION
TELEGRAPH
AND CABLE OFFICE
D.&R.G.W.RR.

Opposite: an eastbound double header stops for orders at Allison, 41 miles out of Durango. There's more activity at Dulce as 499 plows through the May atmosphere to touchdown at the station. Nosecone technology was in its infancy. Years earlier, one of Pagosa Lumber Company's lines connected here. For part of 1951, a Chama-Dulce passenger train was operated on the old San Juan Express timetable until New Mexico approved the end of passenger service in that state. A one-coach train backed four miles to Lumberton where it could wye for the return to Chama.

This page: after the Pagosa Springs branch was discontinued in 1935, Pagosa Junction was renamed Gato, the Spanish word for *cat,* as was appropriate for its location on Cat Creek. Built of logs in 1881, the station was moved here years earlier from Amargo, 23 miles east. The mortar-chinked walls were pockmarked by bullets from some of the wilder moments. Below, an engine check at Ignacio.

Because of the Rio Grande's competition with the South Park, Gunnison ended up with two narrow gauge stations. Each was substantially built, however the South Park's cut stone depot was smaller. Perhaps this was a realistic appraisal of the smaller role the South Park would play in Gunnison affairs. The Baldwin branch passed in front of the station and, although the line had been cut back two miles to Castleton in 1946, this day in May of 1955 saw the tracks cut back even farther. The crossarm-like clothesline and the highchair at the door reveal the building's use as a dwelling.

Upper left: the yellow aspens of September have turned Sublette into a beauty spot. Not a town, but at least an unpaved road ended here. With little else to do with spare time, the section man has the property in immaculate condition. Above, Cumbres Pass in freight train days. The standpipe beside the caboose was fed by a tank out of the picture to the left. The snowshed covers a leg of the wye used for turning helper engines. Cumbres station was closed in April, 1950. The Continental Divide does not pass through here, but instead intersects the railroad at the top of a rolling crest twenty-five miles farther west. Near that point is Monero station, seen at left, whose elevation is 7252, over half a mile lower than Cumbres.

The Gunnison of old served the engines that worked the Salida-Montrose part of the original mainline as well as branches to Lake City, Baldwin, Crested Butte, and Quartz. But the Gunnison airfield beyond the roundhouse and the bathtub Hudson beside it tell what happened. The roundhouse's stepped construction and smoke vents are clearly seen; the ash pit is located next to the gondola. From late 1950, two stalls were used for trucks and by 1952, a Chevy truck was being used as the yardgoat. Below, a flanger sits outside of the car shop and 489 wears white flags in 1952.

Just thinking of the purpose of a snowshed boggles the fireside mind. Marshall Pass was negotiated through snowsheds from its earliest days. At right, the view from out in the backyard looks across the eastern approach, along the western straightaway, and off into the haze toward Monarch Pass. Station, passing track, and post office all shared the shed's protection. That smoke comes from a locomotive inside the structure. Below, 480 runs light, exiting toward Gunnison.

490 sits outside an important Chama structure, the enginehouse.

Rio Grande
318

THE 1950s OPENED somberly enough. The scrapping of the line through the Black Canyon had been completed barely five months earlier, thus creating the Sapinero branch out of Gunnison and the nearly worthless Cedar Creek branch out of Montrose. Engine and car scrapping, station closings, the end of the San Juan Express passenger and mail service, and no realistically good forecast for traffic completed a hopelessly dismal picture.

Abandonment of the San Luis Valley route between Alamosa and Salida broke the Rio Grande's narrow gauge network into three unconnected areas. First to succumb was the Ridgway-Ouray segment in 1952 and the Montrose-Ridgway remainder was standard gauged the following year. The ten-mile Montrose-Cedar Creek appendage completed the abandonment of the isolated Montrose territory. The isolation was reduced to two areas.

At the end of 1953, Rio Grande's application to abandon service to all Gunnison points was approved after sixteen months of ICC procedure. It would be another sixteen months until scrapping physically began and with the passing of one more year, Monarch would be standard gauged. The second half of the decade concerned itself with one area, Alamosa-Durango-Silverton-Farmington, and barely 250 miles of line.

Only two bright spots appeared in the 1950s: the profitable pipe trains and the popularity of the Silverton train. These two aspects carried what remained of the narrow gauge into the sunset years of the 1960s.

The interplay of light and shadow casts the ten car coal train entirely in shadow. Symbolic enough, for the mines at Crested Butte worked only part time by 1952. The train has just left the wye, heading south for Gunnison. Until 1929, the leg of the wye off to the left climbed eleven miles up Coal Creek Canyon and over Kebler Pass to reach the coal mines at Floresta. The four-mile line to Anthracite once ran off to the right past the station. It was junked in 1947. Left: 318, crossing the Uncompahgre River between Montrose and Ridgway, hustles some empty ore cars south to Ouray.

318 generally served the Ouray branch because of weight restrictions south of Ridgway. A mudhen was kept at Montrose for ore and livestock shipments brought into Ridgway by the Rio Grande Southern, but after September 1951, that traffic no longer existed. Thursday was Ouray day, but not necessarily every week since it depended on the amount of ore to be shipped out. Inbound mining supply traffic was negligible. Although Ouray abandonment occurred in 1952, the clean-up train didn't run until the following March and the Montrose-Ridgeway standard gauge conversion took place that July. Right: at Ouray, August 1952.

The Rio Grande dressed up the 268 in yellow as the *Montezuma* for display in the 1949 Railroad Fair in Chicago. When the fun was over, 268 went back to work still decorated, but not named. During 1952, the engine handled the regular once-a-week service to Sapinero. Principal traffic was fluorspar and lumber. Left, in the canyon along the Gunnison; below, just east of Sapinero.

Having received ICC permission to abandon the Gunnison country, the Rio Grande began the massive clean-up operation. Recovery and return of the narrow gauge freight cars was important, not only from the standpoint that they had a sale value of at least $400 each, but also because the ones in best condition were needed to alleviate an equipment shortage that had developed on the Alamosa-Farmington runs.

On opposite page, 268 is found doing the clean-up chores. The top left picture best captures the mood: smoke swirling to taint the cloud-filled sky, then curling downward in cusps among the cottonwoods. The outfit car served as the caboose, but the pilot was a more pleasant place to ride. That had been the battle station for the men throughout the day as they jumped down to remove rocks, set switches, couple cars, and handle the quantity of sand that was needed for traction on the weedgrown sidings. Then, below, the hard day's work was nearly done, but it was decided to reload the sand dome before going up into the engine service area. The fourth man, unseen at the front, wrestles the bag toward the engineman waiting on the pilot. The view shows the auxiliary air tank and the suction pump apparatus for drawing water from creeks when necessary.

In classic pose, the engineer brings out some box cars on this trip. Regrouped at Gunnison, the box cars get dragged over Marshall Pass, right, for the last time. The 480 has been momentarily spared from duty at Monarch.

This was the Gunnison scene as clean-up neared the end. The 480 is coaled by hand preparatory to taking the empties over Marshall Pass. In the background, 268 steams away to scour the branches for some more strays.

With clean-up complete, scrapping might have commenced except that the winter of 1954–1955 was close at hand. The job would have to wait until Spring. The actual awarding of the contract was not done until April 4, 1955 when it went to the Brinkerhoff Brothers of nearby Rico. The Brinkerhoffs had become expert in the grisly business of ripping out narrow gauges. They had scrapped the Rio Grande Southern, starting just three miles north of their hometown in September of 1952. Much of that line was scrapped in steam power, but in the process they adapted a Galloping Goose for scrapping operations. It proved to be well suited for use where lightly constructed rail lines had badly deteriorated. When the Rio Grande Southern job was done, the Brinkerhoffs found themselves at work for the Rio Grande scrapping the ten miles of line from Ouray to Ridgway in August of 1953. From there, they moved on and scrapped the Cedar Creek line that November.

Preparations for Gunnison were made during April. The ex-RGS scrapping goose was brought over and a special winch car and framing rigs were devised for handling the rails on steam-powered gondola trains. By the first week of May, all was in readiness.

Right: 489 wheels a long string of scrap rail cars through Sargent. The Chevy yardgoat is barely discernible off to the right.

Thursday, May 5, 1955 was the day the first blows were struck. The contractor had hired a number of Western State College students for the summer. Things were tried out and the calluses were started with a little exercise in Gunnison yard. Matters would then move quickly to the branch lines. Goose 7 was built in 1936 from a ten-year old Pierce-Arrow and powered by a brand new Ford V-8 engine. The poor goose never sported the frog-eyed fenders nor the graceful archer on the hood ornament that were Pierce-Arrow's pride.

The team breaks loose the rail while the cable sling is pulled back over the chute for the next pair of rails to be loaded. Lots of pictures would be taken of the scrapping operation and the foreman hasn't quite adjusted to that yet. This page: up they go, two-at-a-time. The guider uses a gloved hand in the top photo, but it's better to use a staff as in the lower picture. The sixth crew member operates the little gasoline powered winch. Not too many, fellows, that's close to ten tons already loaded.

Baldwin branch was first to go. The new rig was able to do between a half and one mile per day, so that by June 3 the Baldwin job was done. These two views were taken in the second week of May, one crossing Ohio Creek toward rail's end on a Spring morning supreme, the other backing down that afternoon. The winch on this arrangement was well laid out and substantially built.

By September, scrapping had reached the western flank of Marshall Pass. Up the hill they come, whoopee on the pilot and whoopee in the sky. There was, however, a lot less whoopee the day after Shawano tank, seen above. It had been hot work that day and the crew drank water from the tank, an imprudent thing to do. They all got sick.

Opposite: **489** heads the scrap train inside Marshall Pass snowsheds. The sheds were not a part of the Brinkerhoff contract; they were salvaged by others.

The storage siding at the west portal of the sheds is gobbled up quickly and, at Doyle, the **489** escorts some empties back for another load.

The wind whips the smoke from 489 on September 9, 1955. Scrapping has proceeded now to the east portal of the Marshall Pass snowsheds, adjacent to the pole yard. This was the ready supply of the main supports should the sheds be damaged by fire, wind, or weight of snow.

Down the hill comes the scrap. Cut stone abutments were unusual on the narrow gauge. This is at milepost 225.45, a half mile on the Salida side of Mears Junction. The trick was to get the train stopped at Poncha Junction, because the Rio Grande kept the switch locked until they were ready to move the cars to Salida.

DEVELOPMENT of the gas and oil reserves in the San Juan basin expanded rapidly as the 1950s opened. Drilling operations required substantial amounts of pipe, a bulky commodity from the mills at Pueblo that was destined for remote areas. Shipped by standard gauge over La Veta Pass, the pipe arrived at Alamosa where it was stored and transshipped via narrow gauge.

Farmington was to become the busiest agency on the narrow gauge. Additional track was laid there and at Aztec for handling what was to be an immense increase in traffic. Daily freights were operated Alamosa-Farmington through the winter of 1950–1951, a sharp contrast from the usual wintertime traffic.

Most pipe sections exceeded the 31-foot length of the narrow gauge gondolas. This required flat cars as idlers to accommodate the overhang. A major difficulty arose over the tendency of the flat cars to buckle whenever the trains made a quick or uneven stop. Starting about 1953, the Rio Grande settled on two workable approaches to solve this problem. One arrangement was to convert stock cars which had their draft gear more nearly at deck level and strengthen them with rail sections bolted on like side sills. The other was to cut down standard gauge box cars that had steel underframes.

The end came quickly when the limits of the field were reached. As early as 1955, some pipe was moved in by truck and even though 1956 was still a busy year, trains were down to two a week by 1958. With only twenty runs having been made west from Alamosa in 1966, the Rio Grande asked to abandon on September 18, 1967.

It's starting to get late in the afternoon and 486 has been helping to bring this pipe train up toward Cumbres all day long. The cars in front are the old truss-rodded war horses, those in back have steel underframes. This is Los Pinos, so there's about five more miles to reach the summits.

Top left: a double header pulls some pipe cars through Monero where the route resembles the flight of the proverbial gooney bird. Above, empty pipers being returned up the hill from Chama beside the Cumbres road. Below, 488, cantering along toward Farmington in smoke signal country, sends a few bituminous bulletins to the Ute scouts.

The Rio Grande also ran a pipeline on wheels. Oil from the Blanco basin fields north of Chama was piped to the loading racks in the Chama yard. From there, a fleet of 56 tankers carried the oil to the Oriental Refinery in Alamosa. These cars belonged to the Union Tank line and were of two main types, the older of which dated from 1908 and had an I-beam frame that supported the tank. The newer cars were structurally integrated. Shipments ran in the range of thirty carloads per month and it was this small volume and the obsolescence of the refinery that brought the operation to a close in September, 1964. Sixteen of the older tankers had already been shipped to the White Pass & Yukon, seventeen were scrapped in 1963, and the rest were scrapped at La Jara in 1965. The original owner of the business was Lafayette Hughes whose grandchildren always knew which cars belonged to Gramps — he had them lettered that way.

491 brings both types of tankers around the big curve at Los Pinos on the way back to Chama. Some loaded tankers get a push up the four percent by 473. The front of the train has just about reached Coxo as the caboose clears the Cumbres road.

THE PUBLIC saved the Silverton. They saved a branch line whose magnificent scenery and colorful history might otherwise have suffered the fate that economics once held for it. It took the decade of the 1950s and a little more to resolve the matter.

After World War II, the Rio Grande tried to generate some tourist traffic to offset declining revenues from Silverton's mines. Their program of dressed-up engines, colorful paint, a special all-glass observation car, and more trains did increase the passenger traffic, but not much and not enough.

In the face of losses, rock slides, and washouts, the railroad sought permission to abandon. During hearings, the basic attraction was retained in case a non-profit organization could take over the operation. Meanwhile, the Silverton was becoming unique, better known, and busier. Busier was the key, but business can't flourish on a maybe-not-next-year basis.

All avenues for disposing of the property were closed by the ICC in 1962. In good grace and to the Rio Grande's immense credit, the railroad made the new investments that were necessary to safeguard and expand the business. When the Rio Grande was given a historical association award for that effort, president Aydelotte remarked that in all candor, the award should go to the ICC.

Perhaps. Perhaps the railroad earned it, or perhaps the award should go to the citizen groups, or the voters, or just maybe it was the public who is deserving. Their patronage is what really made the preservation of the Silverton possible.

From high in Animas canyon, the Silverton train is seen pinched between potential rock slides and potential flooding. The first car is the *Alamosa,* a private car that was converted to a coach in March 1957. Opposite: every available piece of equipment that could carry people was pressed into service for the 1955 Memorial Day weekend trip of the Rocky Mountain Railroad Club. Railfans all, their interest in the narrow gauge is no greater than that of average tourists at this dramatic spot above the River of Lost Souls.

Hollywood came to Durango. The wild west scenery and authentic equipment of yesteryear were the exact requirements for some real pot boilers. *Texas & Rio Grande, Around the World in 80 days,* and *Tomahawk & Western* are typical of the films that used the narrow gauge. While lacking certain true life railroading details that railfans enjoy, they've nevertheless brought the narrow gauge to late night TV. 315 with funnel stack appeared in *Colorado Territory,* a 1949 film. But the greatest of all is *Denver & Rio Grande,* a Parmount release of 1951. The 345, seen alive and well next to the foundry in 1950, met its end the following July 17 in a head-on collision that was staged for the cameras. Don't miss it.

The Alamosa shops turned outfit coach 313 into the *Silver Vista* in 1948. Designed for maximum visibility, it regularly traveled as the rear car on the Silverton. An unfortunate car shop fire at Alamosa in September 1953 destroyed this one-of-a-kind. Opposite page shows top, right, and left views. The mudhen wearing Yogi Berra's number is really 453 renumbered for *Three Young Texans* and the station-side lettering on 284 is for *Texas & Rio Grande.*

Rio Grande

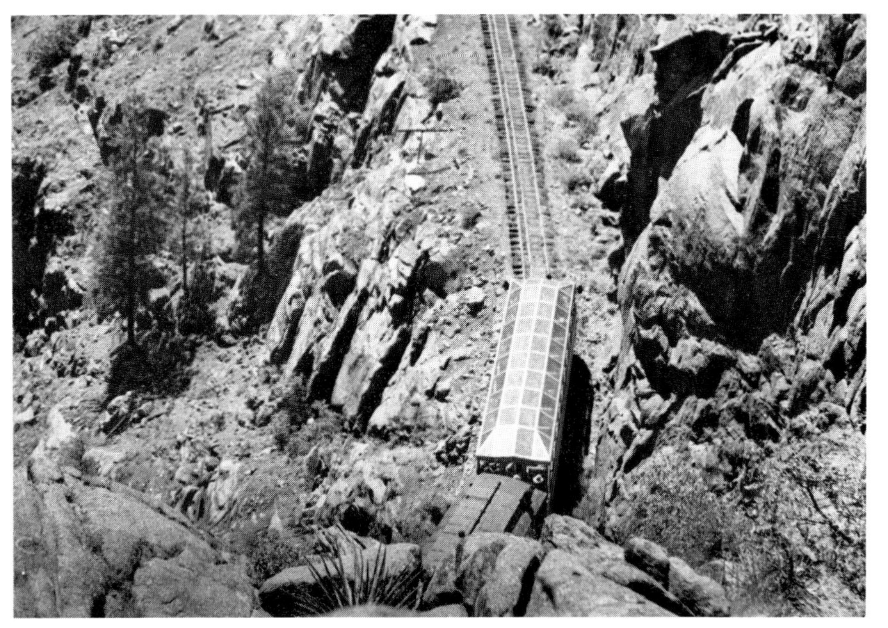

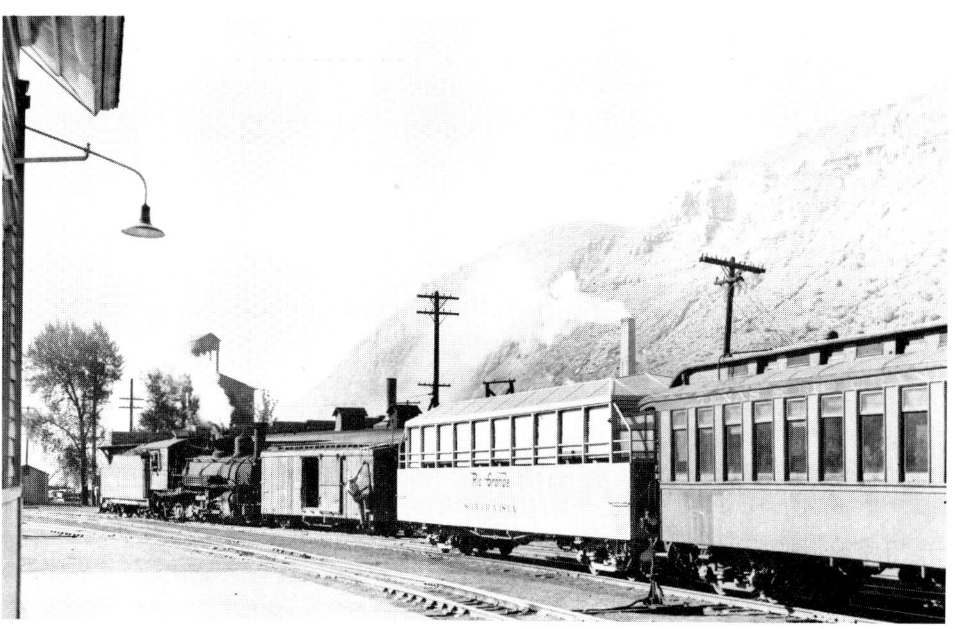

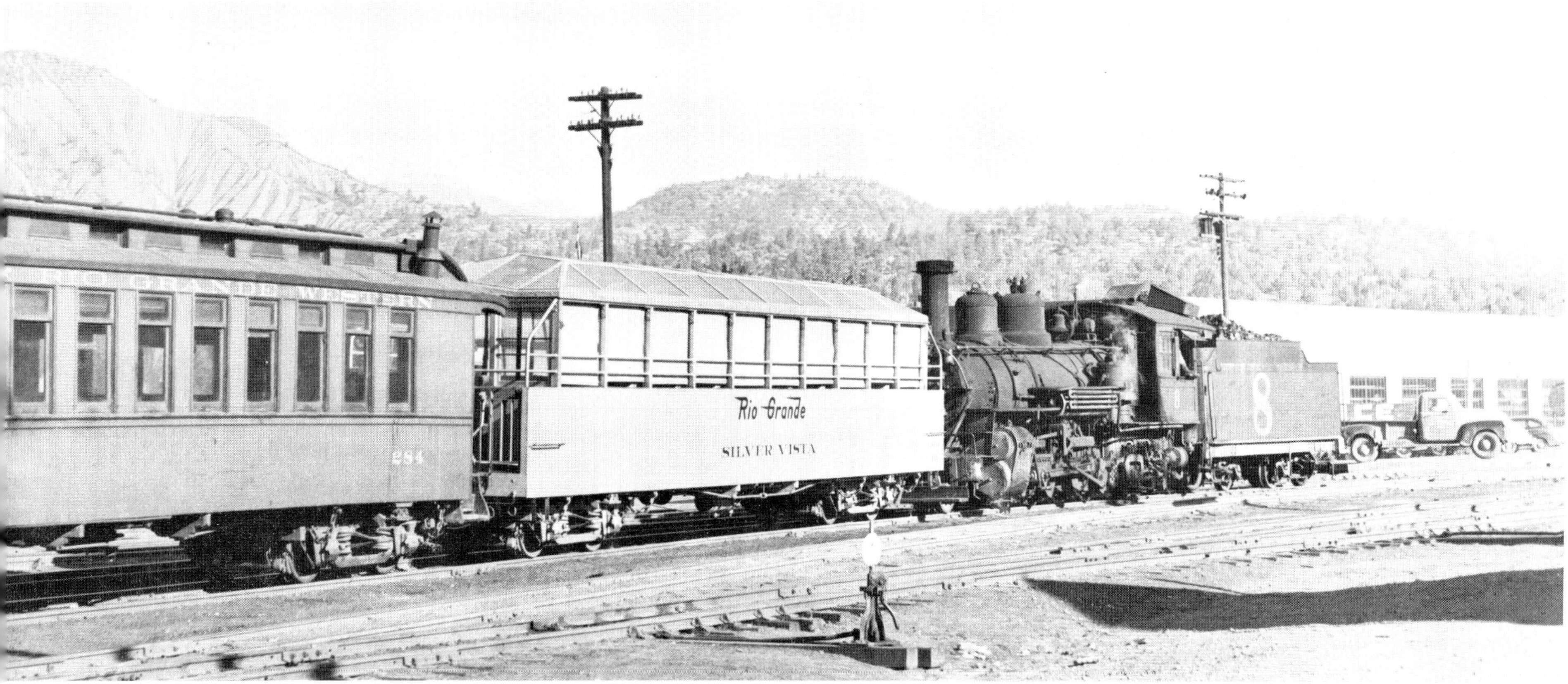
RIO GRANDE WESTERN
284
Rio Grande
SILVER VISTA
8

The Cumbres & Toltec Scenic Railroad, CATS for short, is a child of the 1970s, an active youngster that has come on another day — a day after the twilight on the narrow gauge. The sun had set only to rise again. No history-minded admirer of the Southwest would care to leave the subject of narrow gauge railroading without this epilog.

The sequence of events that brought CATS into being was a zigzag course, largely through the halls of government. The Rio Grande appeared at the ICC in 1967, unable to sustain an antique railroad plant in the face of a then-departed freight business. The National Park Service, the legislatures of Colorado and New Mexico, governors, senators, and representatives were all a part of the consensus making and general arrangements that would be needed to save the narrow gauge. The efforts and intentions were translated into reality in 1970.

From the valleyland at Antonito, through tunnels, past Toltec Gorge, over the summits where 400 inches of snow fall each year, and into Chama run the rails of CATS. For those who would dare hope to ride the route of the legendary San Juan Express, see a rotary fling the snow, or see and hear a string of narrow gauge freight cars underway, this is the place. Apparently the world finds this agreeable too, for each year both Silverton and CATS further develop themselves as major tourist attractions.

This CATS scene is at Juke's tree, so-named because it frequently appeared in photos taken sixty years ago by Fred Jukes. Rotary OM is unchallenged by the snow here, but Cumbres lies ahead.

1976 photograph by Tom Kelcec